CW00520323

FRANCIS FRITH'S

TOWN&CITY

MEMORIES

SKEGNESS

WINSTON KIME is a native of Skegness and has lived there almost all his life. A retired local government officer, he has spent many years researching the history of his town and neighbourhood and has published a number of books on the subject, as well as scores of articles in newspapers and magazines. In 2000, the Town Council awarded him the rare distinction of Honoured Citizen of Skegness for his services to local history.

FRANCIS FRITH'S

TOWN&CITY

MEMORIES

SKEGNESS

WINSTON KIME

FRANCIS FRITH'S
TOWN & CITY
MEMORIES

First published as Skegness, A Photographic History of your Town
in 2001 by Black Horse Books, an imprint of The Francis Frith Collection
Revised edition published in the United Kingdom in 2006 by
The Francis Frith Collection as Skegness, Town and City Memories
Limited Hardback Edition ISBN 1-84589-124-4
Paperback Edition ISBN 1-84589-125-2

British Library Cataloguing in Publication Data

Skegness
Town and City Memories
Winston Kime

The Francis Frith Collection®
Frith's Barn, Teffont,
Salisbury, Wiltshire SP3 5QP
Tel: +44 (0) 1722 716 376
Email: info@francisfrith.co.uk
www.francisfrith.co.uk

Printed and bound in England

Front Cover: **SKEGNESS, SOUTH PARADE 1899** 44346t
The colour-tinting in this image is for illustrative purposes only,
and is not intended to be historically accurate

FRANCIS FRITH'S
TOWN & CITY
MEMORIES

CONTENTS

THE MAKING OF AN ARCHIVE

Francis Frith, Victorian founder of the world-famous photographic archive, was a devout Quaker and a highly successful Victorian businessman. By 1860 he was already a multi-millionaire, having established and sold a wholesale grocery business in Liverpool. He had also made a series of pioneering photographic journeys to the Nile region. The images he returned with were the talk of London. An eminent modern historian has likened their impact on the population of the time to that on our own generation of the first photographs taken on the surface of the moon.

Frith had a passion for landscape, and was as equally inspired by the countryside of Britain as he was by the desert regions of the Nile. He resolved to set out on a new career and to use his skills with a camera. He established a business in Reigate as a specialist publisher of topographical photographs.

Frith lived in an era of immense and sometimes violent change. For the poor in the early part of Victoria's reign work was a drudge and the hours long, and ordinary people had precious little free time. Most had not travelled far beyond the boundaries of their own town or village. Mass tourism was in its infancy during the 1860s, but during the next decade the railway network and the establishment of Bank Holidays and half-Saturdays gradually made it possible for the working man and his family to enjoy holidays and to see a little more of the world. With characteristic business acumen, Francis Frith foresaw that these new tourists would enjoy having souvenirs to commemorate their days out. He began selling photo-souvenirs of seaside resorts and beauty spots, which the Victorian public pasted into treasured family albums.

Frith's aim was to photograph every town and village in Britain. For the next thirty years he travelled the country by train and by pony and trap, producing fine photographs of seaside resorts and beauty spots that were keenly bought by millions of Victorians.

THE RISE OF FRITH & CO

Each photograph was taken with tourism in mind, the small team of Frith photographers concentrating on busy shopping streets, beaches, seafronts, picturesque lanes and villages. They also photographed buildings: the Victorian and Edwardian eras were times of huge building activity, and town halls, libraries, post offices, schools and technical colleges were springing up all over the country. They were invariably celebrated by a proud Victorian public, and photo souvenirs – visual records – published by F Frith & Co were sold in their hundreds of thousands. In addition, many new commercial buildings such as hotels, inns and pubs were photographed, often because their owners specifically commissioned Frith postcards or prints of them for re-sale or for publicity purposes.

In order to gain some understanding of the scale of Frith's business one only has to look at the catalogue issued by Frith & Co in 1886: it runs to some 670 pages. By 1890 Frith had created the greatest specialist photographic publishing company in the world, with over 2,000 stockists! The picture on the right shows the Frith & Co display board on the wall of the stockist at Ingleton in the Yorkshire Dales (left of window). Beautifully constructed with a mahogany frame and gilt inserts, it displayed a dozen scenes.

POSTCARD BONANZA

The ever-popular holiday postcard we know today took many years to appear, and F Frith & Co was in the vanguard of its development. Postcards became a hugely popular means of communication and sold in their millions. Frith's company took full advantage of this boom and soon became the major publisher of photographic view postcards.

Francis Frith died in 1898 at his villa in Cannes, his great project still growing. His sons Eustace and Cyril continued their father's monumental task, expanding the number of views offered to the public and recording more and more places in Britain, as the coasts and countryside were opened up to mass travel. The archive Frith created continued in business for another seventy years. By 1970 it contained over a third of a million pictures of 7,000 cities, towns and villages. The massive photographic record Frith has left to us stands as a living monument to a special and very remarkable man.

This book shows Skegness as it was photographed by this world-famous archive at various periods in its development over the past 150 years. Every photograph was taken for a specific commercial purpose, which explains why the selection may not show every aspect of the town landscape. However, the photographs, compiled from one of the world's most celebrated archives, provide an important and absorbing record of your town.

PRELUDE

Skegness is much older than the Domesday Book. Its name is derived from the Danish, and means 'Skeggi's headland,' although there was a haven town here in Roman times. That Skegness, known to the Romans and the Vikings, was swept away by the tide in 1526 and lies under the sea perhaps three-quarters of a mile from the present shore.

In 1801, the rebuilt village had a population of only 134, with a further 221 in the adjoining parish of Winthorpe. The inhabitants gained a living grazing sheep and cattle on the rich pastures of the marsh, between the Wolds and the sea; there were a few inshore fishermen, and other villagers attended to the sea bathers. Bathing was restricted almost entirely to the wealthier classes, who had taken up the fashion for the seaside which had been set by royalty on the south coast; the Lincolnshire squires drove to Skegness, Mablethorpe and Freiston Shore to keep in the swing. The Skegness Inn (later the Vine Hotel) and the New Inn (Hildreds Hotel) and a number of lodging houses catered for the visitors, but it was only when the railway arrived in 1873 that the sea rather than the green fields provided the village's main source of income.

The Great Northern Railway began running Sunday excursions from the towns and cities of the East Midlands, and Skegness struggled to cope with the boisterous hordes who thronged the High Street on their way to the shore. There was nothing at Skegness but the sands and the sea and the invigorating air, and the village was hard put

DONKEY RIDES C1960 S134110

Here we see plenty of donkeys and riders. Note the two portable ramps with iron wheels, which were used to help passengers get in and out of the pleasure boats.

Prelude

to feed the multitudes and keep them out of mischief.

Almost all the land and farm holdings in Skegness belonged to the Earl of Scarbrough, who resided at Sandbeck Park near Rotherham, and had other estates in Lincolnshire and nearby counties. In the 1870s, agriculture was going through a difficult time, and with the coming of the railway, Lord Scarbrough decided to develop Skegness as a model watering place. It would obviously be an expensive enterprise and demand considerable outlay, but the long-term prospect appeared to make it a sound investment. Work began in 1877, and the next five years saw the tiny coastal village overlaid with wide, tree-lined avenues (51770, page 12), a new main street, promenades and villas and houses to suit all classes. New residents began pouring in to open businesses or work on the construction, and the trains continued to fill the growing town at summer weekends, as well as bringing in more staying visitors.

'And then the donkeys! Who can imagine a seaside resort without its herd of gaily caprisoned 'mokes'? Neddy's perennial face appears everywhere, surely nowhere better represented than at Skegness'.
E A Jackson, 'Skegness and Neighbourhood: A Handbook for Visitors' (1883).

DONKEY RIDES ON THE BEACH C1955 S134109

PRELUDE

LUMLEY AVENUE 1904 51770

Lumley Avenue, with its chestnut trees and wide verges and roadway, is typical of the streets comprising the original grid lay-out of the Earl of Scarbrough's 1870s town plan. The parish church stands in Powletts Circus at the far end. The house on the extreme left belonged to G J Crofts, who could look down the street and see customers entering his large drapery shop in Lumley Road.

The development of the late 1870s saw an entirely different Skegness replacing the old village, which used to straggle along the High Street and Roman Bank. The new main street, Lumley Road - taking the family name of the Earls of Scarbrough - ran parallel with the old High Street, and soon became built up with shops and lodging houses; the Lion Hotel (44354) stood at the western end, where Lumley Road joined Roman Bank.

Across the road, was James Barlow, 'family grocer and provision merchant', and Rowley the ironmonger.

White's Lincolnshire Directory, 1882, also lists the following shops in Lumley Road: bakers, butchers, greengrocers, florists and fruiterers, newsagents and stationers, chemists, jewellers and watchmakers, wine and beer merchants, fancy repositories (gift shops), refreshment rooms and lodgings.

The Lion opened in 1881 with Samuel Clarke its first landlord. He also built the inn, as well as a number of other structures, including the former Estate Offices on Roman Bank. Clarke was also a farmer, a coal merchant and a haulage contractor; he was a busy worker, ready to

LUMLEY ROAD 1899 44354

When the Lion Hotel opened in 1881, the stone lion was placed on the roof above the corner entrance. Across the road James Barlow, 'family grocer and provision merchant,' had the biggest food shop in the town; from the open doorway an appetising smell of ground coffee drifted into the street. Rowley's ironmongery shop was next door. The clock tower, built the year of this photograph, can be seen at the sea end of the main shopping street.

grasp any opportunity, like a number of other new people who had moved in to make a better life for themselves.

A unique feature of the new hotel was the stone lion perched on the roof above the corner entrance. It was carved from sandstone by Richard Winn of Grimsby (1823-1912), brother of Henry Winn, 'the sage of Fulletby', poet, local historian and parish clerk, who lived in Fulletby on the Wolds for almost a hundred years. The stone lion was conveyed the forty-odd miles from Grimsby on a horse-drawn dray. It eventually became unsafe on the roof, and in 1904 it was brought down to stand on the pavement on the Roman Bank frontage. There it remained almost throughout the century, to the great delight of thousands of small children who could never pass that point without demanding 'a ride on the lion'.

There is a story that one Saturday night at closing time, a party of young rugby players, in joyful spirits after an evening's celebrations, manhandled the six-hundredweight lion across the road to deposit it outside the Lumley Hotel. Residents passing the Lumley next morning could hardly believe their eyes when they saw the familiar lion guarding the portals of the rival establishment! The much-loved emblem disappeared very suddenly shortly before Wetherspoon took over in 1997. For some undisclosed reason, the new owners decided to rename the hotel the Red Lion, although there are a least two others pubs of that name in about half a dozen miles.

Even before the new streets were laid out, the Earl's agent, Henry Tippet, concentrated the main building gang on a stone wall parallel with the seashore forming a last line of defence,

LUMLEY ROAD 1910 62855

When it had become unsafe in 1904, the stone lion on the roof of the Lion Hotel was brought down to stand on the pavement. At the same time, bow windows topped by a cupola replaced the former brickwork over the corner entrance. The corner entrance now belongs to a charity shop and the present hotel entrance is off the picture on the left. Traffic was hardly a problem in 1910, and pedestrians wandered all over the carriageway without any worries.

FROM THE PIER 1910 62844

The north beach with a deckchair hut, bathing machines, and a few wooden seats; in the left background is the end of the 1885 Switchback and the Aerial Flight. On the right is the Sea View Hotel and the Figure 8 Railway.

but primarily to be a retaining wall for the building of the promenades. Limestone blocks were brought by rail from Roche Abbey quarry, which was owned by Lord Scarbrough and situated near Sandbeck Park, his South Yorkshire residence. The wall ran from the north end of the town as far south as Derby Avenue, although the parades never stretched the full extent of the wall at either end. The promenade was protected by robust iron railing with wide footpaths and carriageways, and the land side was quickly built up with lodging houses on the Grand and South Parades.

The extension of Lumley Road across the parade leading to the seashore was called the Lumley Pullover. On Grand Parade was a large and imposing row known as Frederica Terrace, the end building being Osbert House. An 1882 directory shows the last-named occupied by Mrs Julia Clifton's ladies' boarding school, but it soon became the Osbert House Hotel and, in the next century, Butlin House.

Parks, arboretums and pleasure gardens (62857 and 38416, pages 21-22) were an invention of the Victorians, creating green refuges amidst their smoky factory towns and cities. They were also fashionable at seaside resorts, so it was not surprising that pleasure gardens should be prominent on the Earl's town plan for Skegness. The ground, close to the seashore, had been a coalyard at a time when small colliers, or 'billyboys,' from the Tyne dumped their cargoes on the sands, to be carted there. In the summer of 1841, 'upwards of 6,000 tons of coal were landed', according to White's Lincolnshire Directory, 1842.

THE BEACH 1890 26694

Donkeys and ponies stood for hire on each side of the Pullover, which was later to be Tower Esplanade.
Note the child's wickerwork saddle hanging on the palings.

THE EARL'S TOWN

The Pleasure Gardens had lawns and flower-beds, rustic arbours, and a pond, and also a bandstand and a large refreshment pavilion (26677, page 23), as well as ornamental kiosks at both main entrances. There were also turnstiles where patrons had to pay their pennies for admittance. The Pleasure Gardens was renamed the Tower Gardens in the 1920s.

The visitors leaving the railway station had to walk the full length of the main shopping street, or along the High Street, to reach the beach, with great benefit for the shopkeepers. On the sands, the fairground was humming with swings and roundabouts, a helter-skelter and a rifle-range, a photo studio, shellfish barrows, pierrots and bathing machines and, or course, the donkeys. In the shallow water, numerous rowing and sailing boats awaited passengers whilst boatmen, in navy guernseys and peaked caps, touted for trips in the 'Primrose' (62867, page 24-25) and the 'Shamrock' and other small craft. When the tide was out, horses and carts carried the passengers across the creeks to the sea (62868, page 27), and a boatman then assisted them up a portable plank ramp into the waiting boat.

The most dominating structure in Skegness was the pier (51763 and 44194, page 29), which opened in 1881. Like pleasure gardens, seaside piers were a Victorian creation, but Skegness and Cleethorpes were the only resorts on the Lincolnshire coast to boast such a prestigious amenity. The pier at Cleethorpes had opened eight years earlier. The Skegness structure, at 1,817ft, half as long again as Cleethorpes', claimed to be the fourth longest in the country.

Financed by a largely local company, it cost about £21,000. The pierhead carried a refreshment saloon and concert stage, whilst the entrance at the land end had a Gothic style toll-house and trading kiosks (51763, page 29). The central approach from the parade was by a wide flight of steps and two gently sloping ramps for prams and bathchairs, lined with handsome stone balustrading.

THE EARL'S TOWN

Work was rushed ahead to complete the pier for Whit Monday 1881, so there was no time for an official opening, but on the Monday and Tuesday almost 20,000 people passed under the tollgate to stroll along the wooden decking right out into what was then the German Ocean. To many of those visitors it would be their first sight of the sea, as travel from inland towns, in spite of the railway, was still restrained by lack of leisure time and by low wages.

The Pier was Skegness's main attraction for many years, with musical concerts at the pierhead. Another attraction was the resident diver who gave daring displays from the high diving board. Notable amongst these performers were the one-legged divers Billy Thomason and 'Peggy' Gadsby. Sad to say, the diving platform was removed in 1948 to make way for a licensed bar.

The famous Clock Tower commemorates Queen Victoria's Diamond Jubilee of 1897, although it was not completed until two years afterwards. Photograph 44195, pages 30-31, shows the garlanded and flag-decked Clock Tower on 11 August 1899 as it was declared open by the Countess of Scarbrough, supported by civic dignitaries and quite a large crowd. The money had been raised by public subscription to commemorate Queen Victoria's Diamond Jubilee two years earlier. The tower is 56ft tall and has four square clock faces with round dials 4ft in diameter. The raised island and traffic roundabout were formed in 1960, and a £70,000 refurbishment was carried out in 1996 - compare this with the original cost of the Clock Tower a century earlier, which was £550.

THE SANDS 1899 44353

It is low tide, and the swingboats and roundabouts are out of reach of the waves. The two wood and pantile shelters on either side of what was to become Tower Esplanade were useful refuges when it began to rain. The museum ship, the 'Eliza' (right), contained a whale skeleton and other marine wonders.

ENTRANCE TO THE PLEASURE GARDENS 1896 38416

Father and son admire the tidy flower borders and shrubs in what is now Tower Gardens, more than a century ago. The garden underwent a complete reconstruction in millennium year 2000.

THE EARL'S TOWN

Beyond the Pier, North Parade remained no more than a gravel road with a footpath on only one side; by the 1920s the land side of the road was almost in its natural state, with two ridges of sand dunes, overgrown with elder bushes, brambles and sea-buckthorn, interspersed with forest trees and clumps of pine. As no development was imminent at the end of the seafront, the Scarbrough estate constructed a wide asphalt footpath, south to north, with minor pathways leading to the parade, as well as rustic fences and seats. It was called the Park (62858 and 51772, pages 31, 35, 36), although it never really recovered from its natural state: eventually the fencing fell apart and the ground returned to the wild. During the First World War, a Scottish horse regiment camped there for some time; when they began calling it the Jungle, the name stuck. Today, nothing survives. The line of the main pathway is now Park Avenue, and the ground is covered by houses and flats, hotels, the Police Headquarters and the Town Hall.

The Figure 8 Switchback Railway (62862, pages 32-33), a most prominent feature, had been erected at the far end of North Parade in 1908 as the successor to a switchback near the pier which opened in 1885, which was said to be the first in England. The four-seater cars of the Figure 8 were hauled up the incline by an endless

THE EARL'S TOWN

Left: THE PLEASURE GARDENS 1910 62857

This was the entrance from Lumley Road to what is now Tower Gardens, before the frontage was built up with shops and cafés. The notice board advertises John Green's Pavilion Refreshment Rooms.

Below: IN THE PLEASURE GARDENS 1890 26677

At the time of this photograph, the prospect from the Pleasure Gardens then allowed a view of the fairly new Parish Church, but other buildings now obstruct it. The bandstand was demolished in 1938, but is now replaced. The Refreshment Pavilion has become a pub. Rutland Terrace remains on the left; the end of the row, on the right, is now the Masonic Hall.

The Earl's Town

The Beach 1910 62867

Until near the middle of the 20th century, there was plenty of choice for a short sea trip in a rowing boat, a sailing boat, a motor boat or even a speed boat. The seal banks in the Wash were a favourite destination, where hundreds of seals could be seen basking on the exposed sandbanks at low tide.

SAILING 1910 62866

'White Wings' is coming ashore and posing for a picture while still under full sail.

chain, from which point gravity propelled them by hair-raising dips and curves back to ground level under the shelter on the far left of the photograph. The Figure 8 was a real thriller in its day; although it had competition from later and larger switchbacks, it survived until 1970, when it was dismantled. The central notice board in 62862, pages 32-33, indicates that Clements' Royal Entertainers at that time had their pitch on the sands opposite the Sea View Hotel, just past the Figure 8.

Skegness had been a fairly sedate little resort until the railway arrived bringing in thousands of day trippers, and the fairground on the beach (62843, pages 36-37) was set up to provide amusement for these more exuberant but less affluent visitors. The rare outing to the seaside

was a time to enjoy something more exciting than a gentle stroll on the pier, but boisterous behaviour was not to everyone's liking. The fact that these trips took place on Sundays - the workers' only free day of the week - made their behaviour seem much worse, as it roused the hostility of local churchgoers, who at that time constituted a large part of the resident population. As early as 1883, a petition was sent to the railway company demanding the withdrawal of excursions on the Sabbath day, but to no avail. The railway contended that they were there to take people where they wanted to go, on whatever day of the week they wished to travel. The Sunday trips continued to run, and argument raged until well into the next century.

THE BEACH 1910 62868

A cartload of voyagers being returned to dry land after a sail in the Wash. At low tide the cart ride was necessary before and after the trip to get across the creeks between the dry sand and the edge of the sea.

THE EARL'S TOWN

After the rush of building in the early 1880s which saw the emergence of the pier, the Pleasure Gardens, the cricket ground and the indoor swimming baths, the national slump brought house sales almost to a standstill. Not until nearer the century's end did things start to move again. Two fine Golf Links were then laid out on the sandhills at both ends of the town, but in the case of North Shore (62859, page 37) a little war had to be fought before the work was completed. Indeed, the crucial encounter in the campaign came to be referred to as the Battle of Granny's Opening.

Most of the land on the North Shore Estate had come into the possession of Laurence Kirk, a Nottingham solicitor. After building houses on the town end of the land, he decided to use the northern section for another golf links (the Seacroft links had opened some years earlier). Unfortunately, Kirk's land was bisected by what was claimed to be a public footpath: it ran from Roman Bank through the dunes to the seashore at a point called Granny's Opening, a main access for the residents of Winthorpe. Without consultation, Kirk blocked the pathway at both ends with stout posts and barbed wire, causing shock and anger and no little distress amongst the people living on that part of Roman Bank and in Church Lane. One of these people was Samuel Moody, a town councillor and a leading Methodist. Sammy Moody roused the Winthorpers for battle, and on 18 May 1908, armed with axes, pitchforks and wire snippers, the eager troops stormed the barricades and made short work of the hated obstructions. Mr Kirk, of course, was not too pleased, and he summoned the ringleaders for trespass and malicious damage.

The hearing took place at Spilsby Sessions House, and a large number of supporters travelled from Skegness, so that the courtroom was packed to capacity. The main argument centred on the right of way problem; witnesses for the defence deposed that the footpath had been used for more than 60 years without hindrance, while plaintiffs claimed that 'Private' notice boards had once been positioned at the entrances. When all had had their say, the chairman of the bench announced that a right of way had been proved, and that the footpath must be restored to its original form. Laurence Kirk took his appeal to the Quarter Sessions at Lincoln, but the judgement was upheld and Granny's Opening remains a well-used public footpath across the Links to this day.

Left: THE PIER 1904 51763

This was the original entrance to the pier, which was completed in 1881; the side ramps were for prams and bathchairs. Admittance through the tollgate cost a penny, but a bathchair and attendant was 6d and a perambulator and attendant 3d.

THE PIER 1899 44194

The long promenade to the pierhead - about a third of a mile - had continuous seating each side; the tube forming the top rail of the backrest on the south side doubled up as a gas pipe to provide lighting. The full length of Grand Parade can be seen, as well as the central beach.

The Earl's Town

Right: The Pier c1960 S134132

This Art Deco entrance to the pier replaced the original Gothic archway in 1937. It was again completely reconstructed in 1971, when the steps and ramps were removed. The land end of the pier was roofed over soon after the end of the Second World War, but Miss Blanchard's Elite Violet Café (centre), a wine bar and other businesses had opened beneath the pier in the late 1930s. In February 1941 a bomb fell just in front of the café, dropped by one of the frequent nuisance raiders that harassed the town. It was lunchtime, and a number of people were inside, but the bomb buried itself in the sand and did not go off!

The Official Opening of the Clock Tower 1899 44195

THE EARL'S TOWN

Right: THE PARK 1910 62858

The broad pathway on the left was the main route through the Park, leading from Scarbrough Avenue to Sea View Road, and is now the line of the present Park Avenue. The remaining footpaths became overgrown, and the area eventually became known as the Jungle. Billy Butlin cleared the ground on the North Parade frontage in the 1920s to set up his first amusement park.

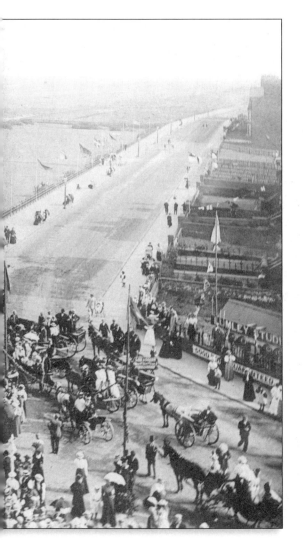

The Earl of Scarbrough's 1870s town plan of New Skegness showed a much larger church, St Matthew's (51771, page 42), replacing St Clement's in the fields (62863, page 40). In addition to giving the land for it, Lord Scarbrough contributed £3,000 to the building fund. The accepted tender was for £7,870, so it left quite a large sum of money to find from a population of little more than a thousand. Numerous bazaars and other fund-raising events were held during the next few years and, by September 1880, the nave and south aisle were completed and services were licensed (38420, pages 40-41). Another five years elapsed before the building was considered to be complete, and then problems began with ground subsidence, which caused the abandonment of the partly-built tower. The Louth architect James Fowler's original plan had been for a tower and spire rising to 130 feet, but a small turret with piped bells had to be substituted (51771, page 42).

John Wesley, as far as is known, never came nearer to Skegness than Wainfleet, where he preached from the Butter Cross on 18 June 1780. His followers, however, are known to have formed a group in the seaside village in about 1820, although it was nearly twenty more years before they were able to build their own little chapel in the narrow main street. The coming of the railway in 1873 brought an increase of members and, two years later, the Wesleyan Methodists decided to build a new chapel nearer the west end of the High Street, which was completed in 1876. The building still stands, though it is now a café, altered and unrecognisable.

THE FIGURE-EIGHT SWITCHBACK 1910 62862

ORDNANCE SURVEY MAP SHOWING SKEGNESS AND SURROUNDING AREAS 1905-1908

THE EARL'S TOWN

Above Left: THE PARK 1904 51772

Here we see the buckthorn-covered dunes in the Park or Jungle; we are looking towards Roman Bank, with bits of the main footpath visible through the trees. The intervening space up to Roman Bank was taken up by horse pastures and allotments. The former Primitive Methodist Chapel can be seen left of centre, and the old white-walled Ship Hotel prominent on the right. The houses on the left are in Scarbrough Avenue.

Above Right: NORTH SHORE GOLF LINKS 1910 62859

The links had opened in the same year as the photograph, on 25 April 1910: the first ball was driven off by the local MP, Lord Willoughby de Eresby. This was followed by a match between four open winners, James Braid, then the current champion, J H Taylor, Harry Vardon and George Duncan. The substantial clubhouse pictured here cost £3,000; it is now the North Shore Hotel.

Left: FROM THE PIER 1910 62843

A late Edwardian scene before development took place along Grand Parade, and when grassy sand dunes filled the space where the Embassy Centre is now situated. Bathing machines stand near the waters edge, and a line of costumes and towels are blowing in the breeze. Funfair rides are also close to the sea. Pleasure boats are anchored in the shallows, and the large hulk of the old 'museum' ship, the 'Eliza', is higher up on the beach.

THE EARL'S TOWN

SOUTH PARADE 1910 62851

The house outside which the horse and cart are standing was where D H Lawrence, author of the controversial 'Lady Chatterley's Lover', stayed in 1902. It was then 'a select boarding house' kept by his Aunt Nellie, Mrs Ellen Staynes; as a teenager, Lawrence lodged there for several weeks while he was convalescing from pneumonia. It figures in his novel 'Sons and Lovers', in which he recalls youthful visits to both Skegness and Mablethorpe. The house is now a private hotel called Woodthorpe, 64 South Parade.

It had been in use scarcely a year when the Earl of Scarbrough began building the new town and, as the population again expanded, it was apparent that the High Street chapel was far too small to seat all the new Wesleyans flocking into the town. The trustees approached the Earl, and he generously gave them a new plot in what was to be Algitha Road (29021, page 43). Like the local members of the established church, the Wesleyans began raising money for their new place of worship, and the foundation stone-laying ceremony took place near the end of 1881. Opening day was on 13 July the following year, and special trains ran from as far afield as Peterborough and Lincoln to bring in supporters and well-wishers. Some voluntary work had been done by chapel members to reduce the building cost to £1,800, but it was quite a few years before the debt was cleared.

The Primitive Methodists also opened a chapel on Roman Bank in 1899 to accommodate their increasing congregations. However, the Baptists had to wait until 1910 before they had sufficient funds to embark on their present building in Lumley Road, which took the place of their little corrugated iron church. Not far from the Baptists, the Salvation Army raised their Citadel in the High Street in 1929, which was replaced by a new church in 1995. The Roman Catholics built in Grosvenor Road, much earlier, in 1898, and that building served them until the present church was built close by in 1950.

Above: WINTHORPE CHURCH 1890 26692

St Mary's Church, Winthorpe is the oldest and finest of the three Skegness churches, dating from the 15th century, and built on the site of an earlier church. It was restored in 1881, but the rich carving of the stall-ends in the chancel is a notable feature. The ancient churchyard cross was restored as a war memorial, whilst the burial ground now serves the whole of Skegness.

Right: ST MATHEW'S CHURCH, THE INTERIOR 1896 38420

Below: ST CLEMENT'S CHURCH 1910 62863

St Clement's Church is a plain little building on the western edge of the town, and was built after the 16th-century flood. Although no longer the parish church, it is still in use, but the cemetery built around it is now closed.

ST MATTHEW'S CHURCH 1904 51771

In the town centre, this replaced St Clement's Church when the new resort town was created in the late 19th century.

Lord Scarbrough's Estate Office continued to administer the foreshore in an orderly fashion, and the reign of King Edward saw no great changes in Skegness from the days of the old Queen. Then came the war, and the peace, and change was in the air. It was a vital moment for Skegness, for the Earl of Scarbrough decided that the time had come for him to get back to his main interests, agriculture and land ownership. The seaside was no longer to be part of his activities, and he offered to sell the whole foreshore to Skegness Urban District Council at the bargain price of £15,100.

The Council held a town referendum on the question, but at that figure there was never much doubt what the answer would be. As somebody has said, it was the sale of the century.

THE WESLEYAN CHAPEL 1891 29021

The Wesleyan Methodist Chapel in Algitha Road was officially opened on 13 July 1882, the fourth of that denomination in Skegness. The three earlier chapels were all in the High Street, the first opening in 1837. As the picture shows, there were few other buildings near this chapel in 1891. The ornate iron gates and railings on the road frontage were lopped off early in the Second World War to melt down for armaments. In the small hours of Sunday 16 February 1941, the church was seriously damaged in an air-raid, and services had to be held in the Sunday School for some time afterwards. The pair of houses on the east side of the building were so badly wrecked in the bombing that they had to be demolished. The former Wesleyan Chapel is now the Skegness Methodist Church.

THE EARL'S TOWN

SOUTH PARADE 1899 44346

On the left is the Sandbeck House Hotel (demolished 1972) with Walter Smyth's wooden photo studio in the front garden. At least three flagstaffs are visible in an age when almost any celebration meant hoisting the flag for Queen and Empire.

THE EARL'S TOWN

THE BEACH 1910 62865

A donkey-man with his metal licence badge prominently displayed poses for a picture with the mother and baby donkey. Will Marsh and his Merrie Men performed in the wooden theatre on the left, near the bathing machines, whilst the fair ground was also near the high water mark with a helter-skelter, roundabouts, a rifle range (right), a photo studio, and lots of other booths where the visitors could spend their pennies.

SKEGNESS FROM THE AIR 1959 AFA78534

THE BIG BUILD

Above: THE CLOCK TOWER 1910 62848

The small parking strip adjoining the Clock Tower contains two motor taxis, a pony trap, a landau and an open omnibus drawn by two horses happily munching away in their nosebags. The amusements are down on the beach, with the old museum ship on the right. Wooden shelters stand on either side of the road to the sea, which was at first named the Lumley Pullover and then Tower Pullover after the Clock Tower was erected; finally, it became Tower Esplanade.

Below: TOWER ESPLANADE C1955 S134120

Landaus still stand for hire in this picture. The flat-roofed Foreshore Centre (left) contained a first-aid room as well as an information bureau, left luggage office and lost children's shelter. It had been built as a dance hall and café in 1911, and was demolished in 1971. Frederica Terrace, on the right, is now extended forward to the pavement with bars and amusement arcades, but at the time of the photograph it was mainly the Parade Hotel.

THE BIG BUILD

Above: THE BOATING LAKE C1955 S134073

So successful was the boating lake, which opened in 1924, that six years later it was doubled in size by an extension south of the big bridge. This picture shows the south extension, near the Axenstrasse; in the centre we can see the Rialto Bridge to the large island, which was replaced only a few summers ago.

Left: THE BOATING LAKE C1955 S134070

The boating lake, with its little wooden rowboats (made by Thickett's, the Grimsby boatbuilders) opened in 1924, the first major work in the great 1920s foreshore development plan transforming what until then had been nothing but sand and dunes.

The takeover of the foreshore found Skegness at a crossroads. The forty years following the initial burst of activity had shown a lull because of the national depression, and then growth was steady rather than spectacular. At the end of the Kaiser's war, however, there was a new surge in population; but Skegness was doing quite nicely and a lot of people could see no reason for much change.

Yet there were other, more ambitious residents who saw the opportunity for Skegness to compete with the likes of Cleethorpes, offering wider appeal with more attractions to bring increased business. The Urban District Council, the new owners, were as divided as the rest of the town, but their engineer and surveyor was in no two minds on the matter. Rowland Jenkins was eager to see Skegness expand, and he had prepared a foreshore development scheme even before the deeds were signed, converting a large part of the sands and dunes to attractive walks and flower gardens, with a boating lake and bathing pool, a theatre and ballroom, bowling greens and tennis courts, and other features attractive to visitors.

After much debate, the scheme was approved in principle and work began with the construction of Tower Esplanade, transformed from the old sand pullover (see 62848 and S134120, opposite). There were a lot of doubters

THE BIG BUILD

THE BATHING POOL C1955 S134128

still, and the firmest objectors were forecasting that Jenkins' Pier, as it was dubbed, would be washed away by the first spring tides. It seemed they might be right, for the winter gales hurled the waves over the partly-constructed esplanade, causing much damage. But this was soon put straight, and when it was completed most people agreed that the new gateway to the sea was a big improvement.

The Council had decided to develop the foreshore piecemeal and the first really big item to be considered was the boating lake, which was to be located amongst the dunes on the south side of the new Tower Esplanade (S134070 and S134073, page 51). The opposition faction aimed to scotch this part of the plan, arguing that not only would the cost be a heavy burden for the taxpayers, but that the lake was not a practical option - the sea winds would continually fill the lake with sand. The Councillors

sitting round the horseshoe table were equally divided; half voted for the scheme to proceed, and half voted for it to be abandoned. The Chairman had to give his casting vote, and the boating lake being at the very heart of the development, the whole plan was in the balance.

The Town Clerk explained the position as the Chairman shuffled his papers, undecided, the chamber hushed in expectation. Then the surveyor got to his feet and explained that, believing approval was only a formality, he had found it necessary to place substantial orders for materials and plant in order to complete the work before the following season. As he sat down the silence was broken by angry Councillors denouncing this totally unauthorised action, and the Chairman's call for order went unheeded for several minutes. When peace was restored, with no more hesitation he cast his vote approving the scheme, whilst handing a severe reprimand to the surveyor for his premature initiative. It was water off a duck's back, the great plan was still alive - but it had been a close-run thing.

Work commenced almost immediately, and the boating lake was officially opened by the Mayor of Lincoln in July 1924. The takings that first half summer were six times the amount estimated. As predicted, sand did blow into the lake and had to be cleaned out, but it was never regarded as a serious problem. The success of the boating lake ensured that the rest of the scheme came to fruition, and each winter found some new attraction created.

The open-air bathing pool (S134128, left and S134033, below) opened on Whit Monday 30 May 1928, and was said to be the biggest open-air pool on the east coast.

Swimming galas were held regularly during the summer season, with races for all age groups, diving competitions, water polo matches and comic acts. The big open-air pool reached its maximum depth midway, opposite the diving platform, with the dual water chute (S134033, centre) at one of the shallow ends. The pool was later partitioned halfway along. Butlin's adjoining funfair can be seen in S134033 with the Big Dipper and the Crazy House. The children's paddling pool (S134036, pages 54-55) was close to the swimming pool as well as the water chute. The men's changing cubicles can be seen across the pool, whilst the ladies' were at the opposite end. The pools were filled in to make a car park after the new, much smaller outdoor swimming pool was constructed in 1999.

THE BATHING POOL C1955 S134033

THE BIG BUILD

The great build on the foreshore took place in about 15 years between the two world wars, and laid the basis for the Skegness of the 20th century. Rowland Henry Jenkins served the Skegness Council for forty years (1912 - 1952) as engineer, surveyor and water engineer. He carried out the foreshore development scheme mostly by direct labour, and also upgraded the highways, the sewerage system and the waterworks, undertaking all this at a time when in spite of national and world depression, the town was making a great surge forward.

The Waterway (S134118 and S134134, pages 56 and 57) took shape in 1931, providing a motorboat service running from the Figure 8 as far as the Pier, and seven years later it was extended to Tower Esplanade. The Sun Castle opened in 1933 with ultraviolet-ray lamps for artificial sunbathing. The sunbathers had to wear special clothing and dark glasses for this purpose and it never caught on, so that only a season or two later, the lamps were removed and the former 'solarium' became just a pleasant spot to enjoy a light meal with light music provided by the popular Florence Andrews trio.

The Pier had altered very little since its opening more than 50 years earlier, but in 1937 an entirely new frontage was built on the parade, very much 1930s style, which was to remain until the present day reconstruction was effected in 1971. The cinema was then at its peak and, in 1933, Skegness had four picture palaces. The Central on Roman Bank and the Parade at Grand Parade had both opened that year to add to the old-established Tower and Lawn, although the latter was to close a few months later.

Lumley Square had been given another facelift, with the demolition of several old houses and their replacement by the gas showrooms (now the KFC café) and public conveniences. Up to that time, all road traffic from Horncastle and Lincoln on the A158 had to turn right on reaching Roman Bank near the old Ship Hotel, and continue by way of Lumley Road to reach the seafront. In 1936, the new Castleton

THE PADDLING POOL C1955 S134036

THE BIG BUILD

Right: COMPASS GARDENS C1955 S134149

In 1930, the so-called Marine Gardens, near the Clock Tower, were properly landscaped to become the Quadrangle Gardens; the name was eventually changed to Compass Gardens, as the giant ground compass with direction pointers was the main feature of the layout. Butlin's funfair and the model yacht pond can be seen in the background, with the old Embassy Centre, built in 1929, on the left. The horse-drawn landaus await passengers for a tour of the town. The large metal object in the centre, painted bright red with white bands, is a wartime mine salvaged from the sea and converted to a collecting box for some worthwhile charity, possibly the lifeboat station.

Below: THE WATERWAY C1955 S134118

Two packed motorboats pass the beach chalets north of the Pier. Later, the chalets were to be rebuilt to face inland, as well as towards the sea.

Below Right: THE WATERWAY C1955 S134134

The boat is just starting out from the north end of the Waterway, with the Figure 8 Switchback, the tennis courts, and the 1930s concrete 'castle ruins' in the background. The motor boat ride still operates, providing a pleasant alternative journey through the seashore gardens from Tower Esplanade to the north end of the parade.

THE BIG BUILD

LUMLEY ROAD 1899 44192

Behind the pony trap on the right we can glimpse Hiley's Restaurant (now the Nat West Bank), noted for its shilling dinners. On the left is the gable end of Hildreds Hotel - demolished in 1987 - and at the centre are what were then the newly-built underground lavatories with a domed ventilator surmounted by a street lamp. They were demolished in 2001.

THE BIG BUILD

Boulevard opened, allowing traffic to drive straight on at the Ship Corner to strike North Parade without having to deviate to the main street. Skegness's first traffic lights had been installed at the Ship Corner two years earlier. Lincoln Road, making another quick route to the town centre, was not to appear for another quarter-century. The old Ship Hotel was demolished in 1936, having been replaced by a new building across the road, and the old ground is now taken up by residential flats, Longhurst House.

In the years between the wars, most of the Skegness shops were locally-owned, and when Woolworths, with their 'nothing over sixpence' range of goods, arrived in 1928, there would be a lot of unhappy scurrying to drop prices amongst existing businesses to try to meet the challenge. Marks & Spencer (nothing more than five bob) did not move into the premises next door to Woolworths until 1937; by that time, Boots the Chemist had already taken up quarters in Lumley Road, to be joined by the grocers Liptons and International Stores. Meanwhile, Skegness Co-operative Society - formed in 1909 with a grocery shop in the High Street - was taken over by Nottingham Co-op in 1927, although the department store in Lumley Road was not built until after the Second World War.

The main street's biggest shops were G J Crofts & Son, who sold ladies' and gents' clothing and a range of furnishing and other goods, and Dutton's Cash Stores,

THE SANDS AND THE PIER c1955 S134119

The pierhead, with the theatre which had replaced the old saloon, or pavilion, during the improvements of 1946, is photographed at low tide.

THE BIG BUILD

THE MODEL YACHT POND c1955 S134064

Close to Butlin's (now Botton's) amusement park, the model yacht pond - opened 1930 - was a popular attraction for many years, with a kiosk nearby for hiring all kinds of vessels.

newsagents, stationers and booksellers, with fancy goods, knitting wool and a lending library. The last-named contained a large collection of well-thumbed volumes, not very frequently added to, costing twopence for a fortnight's borrowing. There was no County Library in Skegness until some years later. The other large shop was Keightley's, a Boston firm, who had taken over Barlow's grocery (now Alison), opposite the Lion Hotel, and they sold a range of goods similar to Crofts'.

There were four banks in Lumley Road, as there are still. The National & Provincial (National Westminster) occupied what had been Hiley's High Class Family Restaurant (44192, pages 58-59), the building opening in 1882 as a reading room and public library. There were not enough residents willing to pay a few coppers for using this worthy enterprise - possibly because so many were unable to read - and it was forced to close its doors. Barclays Bank, Lloyds (Lloyds TSB) and the Midland (HSBC) were all comfortably established in their present premises, although the Midland was not built until about 1921. The site was previously Frith's Restaurant, a building with a curved corner entrance to match that of Lloyds Bank across the street. The new Midland was built in an entirely different style, possibly to contrast as much as possible with their competitors on the other side of Lumley Avenue. Lloyds had opened in Skegness as Garfitt's Bank in the old estate offices on Roman Bank in 1881. Then, as the Capital & Counties Bank, they moved into Lumley Road in about 1911, becoming Lloyds in 1918, later adding another local branch at the former Trustees Saving Bank at Roman Bank as they became Lloyds TSB.

Many of the Lumley Road shops were established very early in the 20th century, and some before then, when their owners moved into the blossoming new seaside resort from other towns. G J Crofts had come from Dorset in 1880, G H J Dutton from Nottingham in 1890, S G Randall, the fruiterer and florist, from Wiltshire in 1880,

George Burley, a tobacconist and hairdresser, from Newark in 1878, Thomas and Henry Marshall, grocers, from Doncaster in 1899, John Green, a baker and confectioner, from near Spalding in 1881, George Morley, a chemist, from the same area in 1874, Freshney and Webb, tailors and outfitters, from Spilsby in 1892, and James Barlow,

SKEGNESS

THE BEACH AND THE PIER C1955 S134150

Children ride over the sands on their donkeys, with the pier in all its splendour in the background. Little more than twenty years later it had been washed away.

grocer, from Somersham, Huntingdonshire, in the 1880s.

The year 1939 had hardly begun when a large part of Butlin's Skegness Holiday Camp was burnt to the ground. Before that summer was over, war had spread over a large part of Europe, leaving seaside holidays and much beside in suspense for six more long and dangerous years. Supermarkets with help-yourself shopping and trolleys and checkouts were still undreamed of, as were yellow lines on roads; at this time, Skegness still had a long pier jutting into the North Sea, fish and chips cost only a few coppers and 'the pictures' were still the most popular form of entertainment.

LINCOLNSHIRE COUNTY MAP, c1850

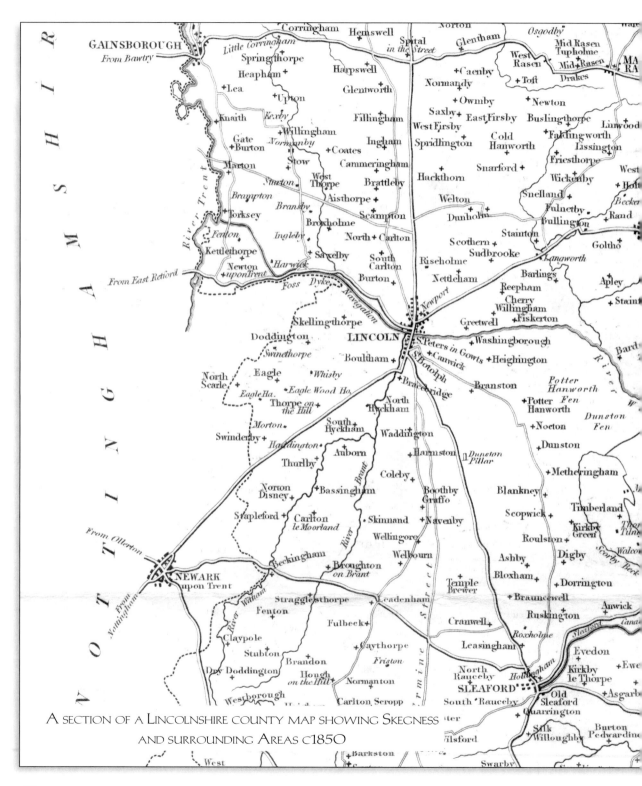

A section of a Lincolnshire county map showing Skegness and surrounding Areas c1850

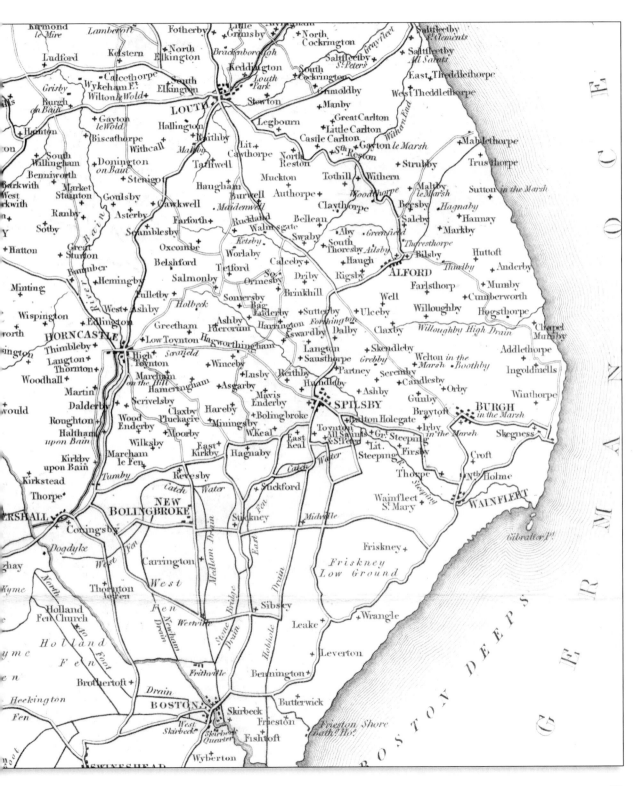

LATER YEARS

Right:
WALSH'S HOLIDAY CAMP c1955
S134102

*Caravan camps have become much
more sophisticated since the 1950s,
but they also had lots of fun in those
days, you can be sure of that! Walsh's
Camp at Roman Bank is pictured
here against the background of the
Winthorpe housing estate; it is still
there, but it has been updated and
has many more caravans.*

Below Left:
NOTTINGHAM CONVALESCENT
HOME 1910 62864

Below Right:
THE CONVALESCENT HOME 1899
44356

at both national and local level. In the decade following the peace it soon became evident that road travel was taking the place of the railways. Up to 1939, the majority of visitors to Skegness still came by train, but in the 1950s more were arriving in coaches and cars. They also demanded greater variety in accommodation, and the old-fashioned boarding and apartment houses gave way to bed and breakfast catering, comfortable guesthouses and hotels, holiday flats and, above all, caravans.

Skegness had had tent and caravan camps since the 1920s, but it was after the Second World War that caravan holidays became big time. By the end of the 20th century the simple 1950s sites (see S134102, left), with their basic provision, had been upgraded with all kinds of amenities and entertainments in an effort to match the large-scale chalet camps like Butlin's. Butlin's was not the first holiday camp in the Skegness area, for the Nottingham branch of the YMCA (Young Men's Christian Association) had established a holiday camp in Grosvenor Road in 1920. Accommodation was in bell tents and ex-army huts, but by 1933 these had been replaced by permanent buildings to become the YMCA's Woodside Holiday Centre, eventually open to all comers.

Until the middle of the 20th century there were a number of convalescent homes in Skegness, for its bracing air was conducive to the restoration of health and vigour. The Nottinghamshire Men's Convalescent Home (62864 and 44356, left) was built overlooking the sea on the buckthorn-covered sandhills at the north end of the town in 1891 with a £10,000 legacy left by Nottingham MP Lt Col Sir Charles Seely. It was taken over by the Nottinghamshire Miners and eventually by the National Health Service, who re-named it Seely House. Photograph 44356 shows the Nottinghamshire Men's Convalescent Home (Seely House) before the later extensions were

T he bombing and the armed services occupation of the Second World War left their mark on Skegness, and when the war ended there was much repair and renovation to carry out. The pressing housing shortage also had to be met, and new estates were built by Council labour at Winthorpe and in the neighbourhood of St Clement's Church, which were supplemented by the quickly erected 'prefabs.'

As after the First World War, great changes came about

carried out in 1933. A similar building was created close by for women, named Carey House. The homes closed in 1978, and were demolished two years later.

Nottinghamshire and Derbyshire have always had strong ties with Skegness and, at the beginning of the 20th century, not only convalescent homes, but also holiday homes for poor children from those counties were being built here at the seaside. There were special convalescent homes for the coal-mining industry of Nottinghamshire and Derbyshire, and also in May 1939 the Derbyshire Miners' Association opened what was then a pioneer venture in the form of a holiday camp solely for the miners and their families (S134007, right, S134115, page 72 and S134192, page 73). Different collieries took it in turns to go on holiday en masse to the Skegness camp, so that whole villages would holiday together by the seaside.

It was situated next to the beach at Seathorne, on Winthorpe Avenue (S134115, page 72). Winthorpe Avenue, leading to the sea, is something of a misnomer, as it was never in Winthorpe parish. Winthorpe was bounded on the east by Roman Bank and did not have a sea frontage. From perhaps the 1930s, the northern end of the Skegness coastal strip was called Seathorne, taking its name, no doubt, from the sea buckthorn, those bright orange-berried bushes with silver green leaves that formerly covered a large part of the sandhills on the Skegness foreshore. The Miners' Holiday Camp adjoined the

THE MINERS' WELFARE HOLIDAY CENTRE C1955 S134007

The Derbyshire Miners' Welfare Holiday Centre, off Winthorpe Avenue, opened in May 1939, a few months before war broke out. Like the nearby Butlin's Holiday Camp, it was a pioneer venture; the miners were determined that their people should be able to enjoy cheap holidays of the same kind.

WINTHORPE AVENUE C1960 S134115

The entrance to the Derbyshire Miners' Holiday Camp and Convalescent Home is on the right, with their gardens coming close up to the pavement. Baker's fancy goods emporium on top of the steps is prominent in this picture.

Derbyshire Miners' Convalescent Home, which had been established in 1928. But only a few months elapsed before war began, the camp was commandeered by the army, and seven weary years passed before the holidaymakers were able to return.

When the abortive Hungarian Rising took place in 1956, many of the fleeing refugees found safety in Britain, and nearly a thousand were accommodated at the Derbyshire Miners' Holiday Centre at Skegness. It was December when they arrived, and they remained there until the following spring, gradually dispersing to work in inland towns. They even printed their own newspaper whilst they were at Skegness, and during their stay the Hungarians gained a knowledge of the new language.

Over the years, the Derbyshire Miners' Welfare Holiday

Centre at Seathorne provided happy holidays for thousands of miners and their families until near the century's end. It was a sad day when the near demise of the coal-mining industry forced its closure and eventual demolition.

The Clock Tower, after a full century, remains the gateway to the seashore. Road traffic swirls round the tower island today, with few visitors failing to pass that way at some stage of their visit. This is in contrast to a century ago (62845, page 79), when the only moving traffic appears to be a pushchair, a donkey cart and one motor car, plus quite a few pedestrians. The immediate surroundings of the Clock Tower have altered considerably over the years. Photograph 44348, pages 76-77, shows rows of boarding houses on the far left along

South Parade. Note the sea wall and iron railings on the left, which are still in place. The grand Frederica Terrace, on the north side (44348, pages 76-77), is now hardly visible. Built in the late 1870s, when it looked over the parade onto the beach, it contained high-class boarding houses, including York House, whilst the end building, close to the Clock Tower, was the Osbert House Hotel (62846, page 78, and 62845, page 79) - the name commemorated an earlier Earl of Scarbrough's grandfather. There was an Osbert Road on the 1874 town plan, but when it was constructed, over 60 years later, it was named Castleton Boulevard after the Earl

of Castleton, from whom the Earls of Scarbrough inherited the Skegness estate.

Billy Butlin bought the Osbert House Hotel in the late 1930s and it became Butlin House, head office for all his holiday camps, hotels and amusement parks, which by then were spread across the country. The building was demolished in 1972, to be replaced by the present less imposing cafés and chip shops. The opposite end of the terrace was not completed until some years later when the Callow Park Hotel was added (62846, page 78, right of the Clock Tower), afterwards called the Jolly Fisherman.

THE SWIMMING POOL, DERBYSHIRE MINERS' WELFARE CENTRE c1955 S134192

The open-air swimming pool at the Miners' Holiday Centre was a popular spot on a sunny day. It had a glass screen sheltering it from the sea breezes. As we can see, the pool had a spring board and diving stage at the deep end and a children's water chute in the shallow part. The large building in the background is the Derbyshire Miners' Convalescent Home.

LATEST YEARS

THE CLOCK TOWER 1899 44197

The new Clock Tower is still garlanded from the official opening ceremony. The bare Marine Gardens stretch along Grand Parade up to the Pier, broken only by the footway leading past the iron fountain to the beach. Walter Smyth's wooden photo studio stands in a front garden on the left.

Hirlap was the newspaper published by the refugees from the 1956 Hungarian Rising who were accommodated temporarily at the Derbyshire Miners' Holiday Centre in Skegness after finding sanctuary in Britain.

LATEST YEARS

GRAND PARADE 1899 44348

GRAND PARADE AND THE CLOCK TOWER 1910 62846

A barefoot boy with a stick guides two donkeys back to their stand on the pullover. The fire-escape ladder propped against the Clock Tower may have been in use to attend the clock face; it appears in that position in a number of pictures of that period. The Osbert House Hotel is on the left of the tower, and on the right is the Callow Park Hotel, afterwards called the Jolly Fisherman, and now amusements.

The central part of Frederica Terrace was formed into the Parade Hotel when Charles Salt purchased the property in the 1930s, but it is now nightclubs, bars and amusement arcades, which were extended right up to the pavement a few years ago. Like Osbert House, they are nothing like as regal as the original building, and are much of a muchness with the rest of Grand Parade as it is today. The only real piece of the old Frederica Terrace remaining is the Ex-Servicemen's Club.

Beyond the almost new and greatly-improved Tower Gardens entrance, the row of three-storey boarding houses (44347, pages 80-81) have long been converted to food and drink establishments. The Parade Cinema has come and gone on a plot of ground between Edinburgh Avenue and Prince Aldred Avenue, where the excursion buses used to park in the 1920s. The cinema is now Plaza Amusements, and the rest of the site has long been built over with night clubs and penny arcades.

GRAND PARADE 1910 62845

More amusements take up what was once Pier Terrace (44201, page 81), beginning with the conical-roofed Pier View on the corner, where the musical Hudsons lived more than a century ago. Richard Hudson moved to Skegness with his wife and children in 1878. He and his forebears were already well-known musicians in his native Preston, and he soon opened a music shop in the High Street. He also formed a band and an orchestra to play on the newly-built pier, and he took a very active part in the affairs of the Baptist Church. One of his sons, George Hudson, established himself as a maker of fine violins, violas and violincellos, which are now collectors' items. Most of these instruments were made at Pier View, which was trademarked as 'The Cremona Workshop'; a George Hudson cello made there was played in the popular television programme 'Antiques Roadshow' on

7 April 1996. George Hudson died in 1905.

Almost across the road, playing in the pier orchestra, a young man was also marked for fame. Gustav Holst, the English composer, born at Cheltenham in 1874, was playing his trombone, possibly in Hudson's or in Surtees Corne's orchestra; it is recorded that 'he scored his Cotswold Symphony in his free time on the sands'. At a later date, the well-known pianist Brian Seymour (1910-98) starred in Ted Dwyer's follies on the pier for 16 years until 1958.

The Pier Hotel (S134086, page 80) was an early product of new Skegness. It opened in 1881, in charge of its owner-landlord Charles Richard Pawson. He was one of twelve successful candidates at the first election of the Skegness Urban District Council in 1894, although he did finish second from bottom on the winners' list. The

LATER YEARS

Left: GRAND PARADE 1899 44347

The Marine Gardens below the iron railings on the left are now taken up by the Embassy Centre and the Compass Gardens, whilst the row of boarding houses on the right are converted to food and drink businesses. The flight of steps through the railings on the left led down to the iron fountain, which is now situated in the Fairy Dell.

Below Left: THE PIER HOTEL C1955 S134086

The Pier Hotel (left of centre) opened in 1881, the same year as the pier on the other side of the road. The large building top right is the Imperial Café and Grosvenor House Hotel. Butlin's amusement park is in the foreground.

Below: FROM THE BEACH 1899 44201

Here we see the bare central beach of a century ago, with no Embassy Centre, fairground car park, Marine Walk and Esplanade, shops, arcades or cafés. Pier Terrace, the Pier Hotel and the Pier itself are there, as well as what was then waste ground between Edinburgh and Prince Alfred Avenues.

Left: NORTH PARADE C1955 S134020

Below Left: NORTH PARADE C1955 S134141

The right side of this picture is now taken up by Natureland, whilst the Figure 8 switchback, the dodgems, the big wheel, the tennis courts and the North Shore Café (right) have all gone. The bushes on the left are part of the grounds of the Town Hall; the building was erected in 1927 as a convalescent home, but it was taken over by Skegness Council in 1964. Further land in the Jungle was subsequently used for the new Police Headquarters in 1974, and then for Lindis Court flats.

Right: NORTH SHORE C1955 S134032

North Shore, or more correctly Sea View, is hardly recognisable in this photograph. The Derbyshire Miners' Convalescent Home can still just be seen in the far distance. The North Shore Café has long been closed, and the helter skelter has also gone. Prince Edward Walk now fronts this part of the seashore.

hotel was originally brick-built; it was only in the 1950s that a total reconstruction left it faced with cement and painted white.

The Imperial Café combined with the Grosvenor House Hotel (S134086, pages 80 and S134020, left) was the first permanent building on that end of the Park, or Jungle, in 1930, but more hotels quickly followed. When Billy Butlin arrived in Skegness early in 1927 with a couple of living vans and three lorries packed with fairground equipment, he persuaded Lord Scarbrough to rent him a strip of ground on the North Parade frontage of the Jungle to set up a funfair. The site is now built over with the County Hotel and there was, of course, no Castleton Boulevard at that date. We can see the County Hotel with its projecting clock in S134020, built for Batemans, the Wainfleet brewers, in 1935. The north ramp to the pier entrance is on the right foreground. Butlin's mushroom-roofed hoopla stalls were augmented by roundabouts and swingboats, a helter-skelter and eventually a roller-coaster. The sea

LATER YEARS

Right: LUMLEY ROAD C1955 S134092

The underground lavatories on the right were demolished in 2001. To the left of centre are Blackbourn's shoe shop and the Nat West Bank, partly hidden by trees.

Below: LUMLEY ROAD C1955 S134062

In the early 1950s, the street lamps were being converted from gas to electricity; these in Lumley Road are the last gas lamps in use just before the changeover. The 'No Waiting' road sign (left) was used during the 'unilateral waiting' period, when vehicles could wait on one side on odd days of the month and on the opposite side on even days. The signs were hinged in half moons so that they could be tipped over to show which side of the road was currently available for parking.

SOUTH PARADE, THE PUTTING GREEN
C1955 S134067

*There is still a putting green near the
Clock Tower, but it is in an adventure
form, and is perhaps not so attractive as
the simplified version was. The flagstaff
belonged to the lifeboat station, which
at that time was sited off the picture to
the right, and a flag was flown when the
lifeboat was at sea.*

CRAZY GOLF C1955 S134051

The Crazy Golf Course is still there; so are the hotels and flats fronting South Parade, including the Lakeside Hotel on the extreme right.

side of North Parade, from the pier to the Figure 8, was lined with bowling alleys, a rifle range, race games, the Crystal Maze and an 'aerial flight.' The last-named was an athletic trip for the punter, who was suspended from a steel cable between two raised platforms, with a safety net below for those who did not make the full trip.

In 1928, Butlin obtained a long lease from Skegness Council to set up a new funfair on the south side of the pier; the following summer he transferred his stalls and rides there, together with those from across the road,

to whom he rented pitches. Butlin retained this big amusement park until 1964, when the tenancy was taken over by Botton Bros, who rebuilt the site from scratch, and they retain it to the present time.

Billy Butlin eventually retired to Jersey and died there in 1980. His last visit to Skegness was to switch on the illuminations in 1977: on that occasion he stayed at the County Hotel, which had been built on the site of his first Skegness amusement park just 50 years earlier.

The great east coast flood of 31 January 1953 saw the tide reaching up to the parade walls and causing immense material damage, but no lives were lost and no houses had to be evacuated. Butlin's Camp, just outside the town boundary, was completely inundated: the sea reached up to Roman Bank, and six lives were lost there. The sea walls from that point northward to the Humber were swept away, and more than 40 people were drowned.

Following the years of war, the 1950s and 1960s were not as free from worry as most people had hoped. After the great flood came the great blizzard of January 1956. It isolated the town by road, rail and telephone for several days, and left the inhabitants with neither heat or light as cables and wires sagged to the ground.

The Beeching axe of 1963 marked Skegness railway station for the chopper, but valiant resistance won reprieve. However, in 1978 there was no defence when the sea devoured the most valuable part of Skegness Pier.

The 1980s saw the shopping area of Skegness greatly improved, stimulated by the advent of The Hildreds in 1986 and the resurgence of the High Street after it had been reconstructed and made into a one-way street. Lumley Road (S134092 and S134062, pages 84-85) began to attract more multiples and is now spilling into Richmond Drive, with more commercial development in that direction. Pubs and clubs have continued to proliferate, and one of the most noticeable changes in the main shopping street has been the influx of charity shops, estate agents and building societies, all now a feature of any town centre.

Compared with the big build on the foreshore in the 1920s and 30s, the second half of the 20th century had little to show, although there was much necessary reconstruction and upgrading of existing attractions which had begun to show signs of age. The new major amenities have been Natureland (1965), Panda's Palace (1986), and Prince Edward Walk and Lagoon Walk (1992). The last named was really a reconstruction, but it was such a vast improvement that we have to count it as a new work. There was also the Festival Centre, commemorating the Festival of Britain in 1951, but it was demolished just 50 years later.

The updating of the seafront amenities and the extension and improvement of the shopping area and the industrial estate are considerable pluses. Although the road access system remains a worsening problem, the future of Skegness, both as a holiday resort and as a residential town, seems assured.

The following people have kindly supported this book by purchasing limited edition copies prior to publication.

Mollie Abbott, Burgh Le Marsh

Michael Abbot, Lincoln Road, Skegness

To Amy with love, Husband Dr Vic Cassapi

In memory of Andrew and Alexander Archer

In memory of Leslie Archer, Husband of Kathleen

Mr and Mrs Armstrong, Skegness

Vern and Myles Bee, Winthorpe, Skegness

Reverend Linda Bond, Skegness to Eileen

Kim and Kevin Booth

In memory of Norman (Redcoat) Bradford

Eric Brewster, Sutton-on-Sea

In memory of Doreen Broadbent

Danny Brooks

Derek Burman, Skegness

Olive and Gordon Cartwright

John Collier

Mrs J Cooper and Family, Skegness

Alan and Sandra Davidson

In memory of Mr and Mrs A G Davies

Margaret Dickinson, Skegness

Beryl Maisie Dimmock and
    Michael John Dimmock

James A Draper, 05/12/80

The Eason Family, Chapel St Leonards

Mr and Mrs R P Eldred, Skegness

As a tribute to our Son, Michael Eldred

In memory of husband Jim Elliott from Jan

Mrs Susan A Farrell

Cicely and Tony Fisher

Derek W Garrill

Heather and Michael Gray

Mr G and Mrs W Gudgeon

Stanley, Jessie, Patricia and Janis Hall

In memory of Mick Halls, Ingoldmells

The Hancock Family, Skegness

Sheila D J Hannam

Mr and Mrs G W Hart

Anne Harvey, Walsh's Holiday Park

Mr and Mrs N W Hawkins

Tribute from the Hayes Family, Winthorpe

Patricia Hayward, In Memory of her Husband

To Thomas Hayward on his 5th Birthday,
    from Nan and Grandad Merriman

Peter Vincent Hedge

Maureen A Holland (Mo), Chapel St Leonards

Alan William Holmes

The Hyde family, Pam's Mum and Dad Tribute

To Ian, love from Josephine, Lisa and Sarah

Mr and Mrs V James, Skegness

E Jenner and Family

In memory of Peter Johnson, Skegness

Alan and Chris Johnson

Ann Barton Kajander

To Keith, Happy birthday, enjoy Skegness, love Sue

To Helen Kennedy from Mama and Grandad

Don and Joan Kitchener, Skegness

To Shirley Locke on her 70th birthday

Tony Mancini

Jack Mapletoft

Barry Marshall

To Mary with Love, Brian

To Mary on your Birthday with fond memories
from Mum

Michael May

Ron and Carole Merrett, Talbot Road

In memory of the Miller Family, Skegness

Councillor and Mrs K Milner

Monsell Hotel, Skegness, PE25 3JY, Tel 898374

John Henry Nelson, Skegness, London, Harare

For my Angel, Nichola, Love from Bunny

Mr Brian and Mrs Ann Old, Ingoldmells

Phillip, Patricia, Wayne and Leasa Olivant

In memory of John Pauline, Burgh Le Marsh

Graham and Marjorie Payne, Skegness

Catherine Pepperell

In memory of Mr Percy and Mrs Mary Cave

Mary Piant, in memory of Peter

Bernard Platts

Antony, Beau and Belinda Puddick

In memory of my parents, John Ranson

Dennis Ratcliffe

Son Geoff Reynolds, Skegness, on his birthday

James Barrie Richards, Skegness

Mr and Mrs R J M Ridout, Skegness

Edward and Joan Salter, Skegness

Sandra and Family, Christmas 2005

Patricia Seaman, née Teeling, born 1947

Colin and Jean Sempers, Skegness

Dean Sharpe, Cairns, Australia

Skegness Standard

In memory of George Derrick Slight

Geoff, Sue, Allison, Rebecca and Charlotte Smith

The Spence Family, Irene, Sheila and Philip

In memory of H E Ted Spence, Skegness

Michelle and Adrian Stennet, Skegness

Mr and Mrs P Stewart

Charles Taylor, Skegness

Jennifer Teeling, born Skegness 1948

Christine Turner

Rita and Alan Twigg and Family

The Wade Family, Skegness

Robert L Waite, Skegness

Maureen Wallege

To Ben and Rachel Waxman, Skegness

Mr and Mrs A Weston

Mr and Mrs M Wheelton, Chapel St Leonards

Helen and Bill White, as a tribute to Alan and May

Mr B Whitehead and Family from Clowne

J J Wilkinson, Skegness

Maureen Wright

Mrs Joan A P Wright

FREE PRINT OF YOUR CHOICE

Mounted Print
Overall size 14 x 11 inches (355 x 280mm)

Choose any Frith photograph in this book.
Simply complete the Voucher opposite and return it with your remittance for £2.25 (to cover postage and handling) and we will print the photograph of your choice in SEPIA (size 11 x 8 inches) and supply it in a cream mount with a burgundy rule line (overall size 14 x 11 inches).
Please note: photographs with a reference number starting with a "Z" are not Frith photographs and cannot be supplied under this offer.
Offer valid for delivery to one UK address only.

PLUS: **Order additional Mounted Prints at HALF PRICE - £7.49 each** (normally £14.99)
If you would like to order more Frith prints from this book, possibly as gifts for friends and family, you can buy them at half price (with no additional postage and handling costs).

PLUS: **Have your Mounted Prints framed**
For an extra £14.95 per print you can have your mounted print(s) framed in an elegant polished wood and gilt moulding, overall size 16 x 13 inches (no additional postage and handling required).

IMPORTANT!

These special prices are only available if you use this form to order . You must use the ORIGINAL VOUCHER on this page (no copies permitted). We can only despatch to one UK address. This offer cannot be combined with any other offer.

Send completed Voucher form to:
The Francis Frith Collection, Frith's Barn, Teffont, Salisbury, Wiltshire SP3 5QP

CHOOSE A PHOTOGRAPH FROM THIS BOOK

Voucher for **FREE** *and Reduced Price Frith Prints*

Please do not photocopy this voucher. Only the original is valid, so please fill it in, cut it out and return it to us with your order.

Picture ref no	Page no	Qty	Mounted @ £7.49	Framed + £14.95	Total Cost £
		1	Free of charge*	£	£
			£7.49	£	£
			£7.49	£	£
			£7.49	£	£
			£7.49	£	£
			£7.49	£	£

Please allow 28 days for delivery. Offer available to one UK address only

* Post & handling		£2.25
Total Order Cost		£

Title of this book . . . .

I enclose a cheque/postal order for £ . . . .
made payable to 'The Francis Frith Collection'

OR please debit my Mastercard / Visa / Maestro card, details below

Card Number

Issue No (Maestro only)   Valid from (Maestro)

Expires   Signature

Name Mr/Mrs/Ms . . . .

Address . . . .

. . . .

. . . .

. . . . Postcode . . . .

Daytime Tel No . . . .

Email . . . .

ISBN 1-84589-125-2   Valid to 31/12/08

Can you help us with information about any of the Frith photographs in this book?

We are gradually compiling an historical record for each of the photographs in the Frith archive. It is always fascinating to find out the names of the people shown in the pictures, as well as insights into the shops, buildings and other features depicted.

If you recognize anyone in the photographs in this book, or if you have information not already included in the author's caption, do let us know. We would love to hear from you, and will try to publish it in future books or articles.

Our production team

Frith books are produced by a small dedicated team at offices in the converted Grade II listed 18th-century barn at Teffont near Salisbury, illustrated above. Most have worked with The Francis Frith Collection for many years. All have in common one quality: they have a passion for The Francis Frith Collection. The team is constantly expanding, but currently includes:

Andrew Alsop, Paul Baron, Jason Buck, John Buck, Jenny Coles, Heather Crisp, David Davies, Natalie Davis, Louis du Mont, Isobel Hall, Chris Hardwick, Lucy Hart, Julian Hight, Peter Horne, James Kinnear, Karen Kinnear, Tina Leary, Stuart Login, Sue Molloy, Sarah Roberts, Kate Rotondetto, Dean Scource, Eliza Sackett, Terence Sackett, Sandra Sampson, Adrian Sanders, Sandra Sanger, Julia Skinner, Lewis Taylor, Shelley Tolcher, Will Tunnicliffe, David Turner and Ricky Williams.